PACIFIC
POWER &
LIGHT

*Michael
Dickman*

ALFRED A. KNOPF

NEW YORK

2024

PACIFIC
POWER &
LIGHT

*

POEMS

THIS IS A BORZOI BOOK PUBLISHED BY ALFRED A. KNOPF

www.aaknopf.com

"Hawthorne" first appeared in *Harper's Magazine* (October 2020).

LIBRARY OF CONGRESS CATALOGING-IN-PUBLICATION DATA
Names: Dickman, Michael, 1975– author.
Title: Pacific power & light : poems / Michael Dickman.
Other titles: Pacific power and light
Description: First edition. | New York : Alfred A. Knopf, 2024. | Summary:
"The award-winning poet returns to his home place in the Pacific Northwest, where the neighborhood simmers with the chemical presence of human trouble, and sparks of beauty coexist with danger. This sound-driven, image-driven collection carries us to the lower-middle-class Portland neighborhood of Lents, where Dickman was raised by a single mother. Here, as a skateboarding boy practices his kick-flip on the street, enlightenment simmers under the surface of both the natural world and the human constructions that threaten it. The rivers shrinking to a trickle, the unaddressed crisis of homelessness, the drug use in a local park: these run side by side with the efforts and structures of families, created mostly by working mothers, with their jumbled bottomless purses and hard jobs; Dickman's own mother worked at the power company of the title, PP&L. His exquisite surreal narratives take us down through these layers, illuminating the way we've treated and should treat one another, seeking integrity and understanding in the midst of a broken world"—Provided by publisher.
Identifiers: LCCN 2023012342 (print) | LCCN 2023012343 (ebook) |
ISBN 9780593536490 (hardcover) | ISBN 9781524712419 (trade paperback) |
ISBN 9780593536506 (ebk)
Subjects: LCGFT: Poetry.
Classification: LCC PS3604.I299 P33 2024 (print) | LCC PS3604.I299 (ebook) |
DDC 811/.6—dc23/eng/20230316
LC record available at https://lccn.loc.gov/2023012342
LC ebook record available at https://lccn.loc.gov/2023012343

Jacket photograph by Ken Hermann
Jacket design by John Gall

Printed in Canada

First Edition

For Carl Adamshick

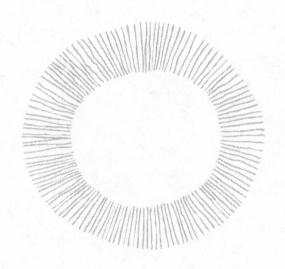

Why not go home?

A. P. CHEKHOV, *THREE SISTERS*

CONTENTS

I

II

III

I

TO A MOSQUITO IN LENTS

Cherry Coke
Sucked up through a metal straw
You look like a line drawing
In reverse

Sketched out in the air

Lay-offs beat kids in parking lots

You don't belong here

Passing saliva
Back and forth on a teaspoon
Compound and cashless

While I eat Cheetos from a single-use bag you carefully lick orange
    feedback off my long and delicate fingers

Ecclesiastical
And hypoallergenic
Getting sick behind the Checkers Mart

There's so much I want to tell you

Slivers from the new bark dust feel good

Needles
Stay dry inside fanny packs
And you keep every promise

HYDRANGEA

From the fridge
Voices and tubs of whipped cream
In cool limelight
Glowing day and night

Against the house
A chain or picket fence all in a line
Imitating kids

Part shade part whipple

Buttercups dust the car windows in weird pollen

Dog hair trims the toilet seat

My headache is native and breaks off in little pieces of ice
    feathered through with yellow comb

Smooth leaves and powdered milk
Icebergs leak flowers
And medical-grade neon

Over-the-counter Jell-O
Open the fridge and the fridge sighs

The petals are the same color as Wet n Wild MegaLast High-Shine

It's terrible here

WARP & WOOF

Hard drugs in Forest Park
Rewrote black-capped chickadees
Recreational networks
And carpet flowers

Wet origami unfolds
Ferns behind a loose
Curve

For weeks I've been having trouble seeing out of my left eye

A woolly sunflower

Mal Waldron
Plays an avalanche or
Maidenhair design

Waves get lumped into a runnel

Dew on the tips of my Doc Martens hangs from a snag

And tracers wriggle to the surface
I can hear it

Knot density in salmonberry

A displaced trickle

*

Tree frogs
Download Lysol into the basalt
And regulated duff

Every few feet in front of me
Grass dilates in a wavery
Grande Ronde

No stems in the rods or cones

The Light Rail scribbles changes through pine needles and green
    polyps

When this eye stops working will another start?

Black-tailed deer hop the fence
Mostly a brown or white
Dust bunny

Tiny dots that move quickly across Thurman Street

Look-alikes

Plugging in a shrub
Puff stitch or a bad cough in the weeds

A place

And people in a place

SWITCHFLIP

A yellowjacket turned
Inside out
A stinger and an instep meet in the middle of the air
I hold my mother's hand
If you land it you live forever

ROSS ISLAND

Holiday of native plants and drive-thrus
On the way to Mrs. A's
Or the Naito Parkway
Soft blue

Blanket in the wash
Awash in surface runoff from a riffle
Stars fries and perch

The older boys in the skate shop could see my underwear

I would do anything for them

Crown shyness
Surrounded by trucks and decks
If I close my eyes I am there

Almost there

Moms on their way to work slip down Powell Blvd. like salmon in
    springtime or haiku

Pantyhose
Stuck to acid green leatherette
Also available in vinyl
And melted butter

They can't yet stick
A backside off a dragonfly
Or crabapple

Lipstick buried in purses and loose grip-tape

It's all they can do

TO MY MOTHER'S DOGS

Sad and in love
With big sad eyes and happy for a scratch
For anything at all
A kind call

Let out into the yard
To somersault
Piss and dig up dried shit

Run unwired circles from one end of the ranch-style to the other
    through attenuated clouds of kids

They kick at sleep and dream

Mom feeds me and fills the bowl dreams
Mom tickles my pink dreams
Mom cuddles and calls

Good for good

Other dreams are blank or unremembered

They chirp at her socks

They look up with people eyes and growl at doorknobs

*

Thin lipped and foaming
Buckets of white joy
Splashed onto fresh lawn
We can't ever know what we're going to be

Shit tufts in strands
Dangle from greased assholes
Riding carpets down
Past dust motes

Even old ones are children

Newborn every fifteen minutes
They cry to see her and eat up
Her pantsuits

Russet scraps dug out of the davenport

Terrified of ammonia and metal tables and a future they can't quite
see to the end of

Their faces are open bodies of distilled water

They can't swim

*

Dislocated
On kitchen tiles and soiled bath mats
Shit-ton excited to see you again

Their smiles
Boiled down to glacé
A crown of ticks surrounds their damp tummies
Fontanelles made of loneliness

Ground beef

Pills hidden in wet food

Their paws are formal and cross at the ankle
Their toenails sound like rain
Tap their cigarettes
And exhale forgiveness

They are cheerful and still alive running from strangers quick
     between legs they skitter and balk

Coats soft in both directions

They don't hurt anybody they need help

HAWTHORNE

Vertical lift
In the Oregon sunshine
Makes for a perennial
Escape route

Black walnut trees are memory and skid

Maples drop green
Helicopters without pilots
Onto accessible sidewalks

A spoonbill or springtail marks a new bike path to the waterfall

A bus stops here
A bus stops there

If it's not one thing it's another

Cabbage whites
Follow me from the Cash & Carry
A flat light beneath the overpass

Beauty and structure without a lot of work

Gladiolas wait for a do-over
And circuit breakers
Pop the truss

The difference between
A moth and a butterfly
Is traffic

Look down trees

It is early October

I walked across the green X-ray grating and did not know where
    I was

BLIGHT OF THE FUMBLE BEE

It comes in waves
A yellow signal before you
Have to sit down

Gold couscous
Neosporin

Carpenters eat out verandahs leaving small piles of sawdust in
    even rows of corbeled halos

Ordinary things are jumpy and change shape

Cherries weep paper snow
It happens all in one day and then they are gone
Imported from Japan

Moshi
Moshi
Mayonnaise heaped onto iceberg lettuce

Here comes a line of ants playing the marimbas

Here comes a curlicue

*

Difficult to focus
On a marigold or daisy
Natural light

Heaves into a Glad bag

Lawns are replumbed and bounce on a line in the breeze
Scrambled eggs
Dazed fairies

Leaf-cutters reimagine the backyard as a carpet of cosmopolitan
    fluff the color of Crystal Light

Sweet'N Low

I wish my head didn't hurt so much
I wish I had
Someplace to go

The driveways here are very short and end in elegy

An astigmatism in the glitchy zinnias

A sine wave in the tamago

*

Hopscotch
Through a flutter of dogs and dandelions
Sidewalk chalk spells out
The last word

A realistic spot right in the middle of the big hosta

I hope I didn't
Kill the polyester I helped
Out of the kitchen

Ms. Fou-Fou is that you?

The oscillating fan turns away at regular intervals leaving a silence
    that is part forewing part hindwing

Something
In the new planters goes
Wiggle-wiggle

The grass in the sun smells like amphetamines

Anton Chekhov smells like honey

*

Ollied over a trance
Between Toyotas in the mall parking lot
I was reborn as exhaust noise
In royal jelly

White denim with gold divots

White cells combed up into a Blizzard or Dilly Bar

It's good to be here

Eyesight multiplied
Compounded into an egg
And dart design

My mother raised me to live inside a sunflower

It opens and speaks

Yalta
In the ova

A pollen brush on either side of us scatters carpels in a pirouette or
    chirashi style

*

No relief
From the family vacation Dairy Queen
A saffron cloud dusts
The new sibilance

We cut through a monotone of cotton suits and summer petticoats

Hamachi is weightless and glistens
Like tapioca

Tweakers
Peel off in sunlight
Our empty pockets

I have wasted so much time

Sweats make their home in the ground and mass provision for
    snacks or float in Dominican amber

A Xerox of a Xerox
Of a samovar

A galaxy on the underside of your checkered Vans

SAFETY PINS

Two blue herons
Downshift in the sun
To preen
The Jurassic fluff
Out their green feathers and white safety pins

LILACS

Hiding in a thimble
Old lace or eggshell spray foam
Works its way into buckets
Of purple popcorn

Naturalized
As shredded pompoms
And mirror glaze

You can feel it all over

Gin and tonic

The bathroom light rinses out a coronet before disappearing into
    Pond's cold cream and Demerol

Swimming in an ashtray
Above a clarified mind
And a coffeepot

Alive on Mother's Day
They don't cure cancer or glow in the dark
They look like cottage cheese and stay up late on the telephone

Tiny birds shit on every terminal branch

I can smell their undies

In the palm of my outstretched hand
Powdered faces and clean
Assholes

GERANIUMS

Their heads are zonal
Fall all over themselves
Then shake their brains out like confetti
In the backyard

Ringlets ladder down
From an event horizon
You can rely on

Leaves unfurl into nothing
Grass unfurls

Great-aunts smoke cigarettes in rollers and folding lawn chairs set
    out on the driveway in the sun

Stare into light-years and can't remember your name

I cut my hair off and listened to No Wave
Verbs in foliage
Scissors in a drawer

A mouse-moth leaves its phone number on the underleaf of a
    dogwood

Streamers
Twist from one corner of the room to the other
Egg yolks stuffed with mustard
And highballs

Tango and citronella

The daytime soaps come on at two

Hanging
All in a row they don't mean
Anything in particular

SUPERIOR FLORISTS

Cut on the bias
Then tied together with pink
Ribbon or silver
Tercets

Daisies are not Monk
Even if you throw in some free
Baby's breath

High on Scotch broom
And whip-its

Wrapped in neon Mylar that reflects a curved edge in space or wet
    newspapers tied up in bad news

Spoon shaped or saucer

They remember what you ordered last year

A child's drawing
Of a yellow flower in real life
Is full of life

*

Bouquet designs
Closer to the end of spring than
Cinquefoil

Carnations live forever
In a carton of milk
Impressed and tend to fall one way
Or another

Jonquils and gamma rays

They turn their faces toward the window and whisper your name

Drinks at the Lotus are coin-op and just around the corner from
    the park blocks and your first thought

A scion of Dee-Lish will make up for lost time

Koko Loko
In a hanging basket does
We meet at Mary's Club

I give Mary flowers

*

Birds talk
Nonchalant and peel off
Into green blurs

A queen bee crosses the Rose Quarter

Teleflower
Petal effect
Runs through the neighborhood

Foam and glitter on hot sidewalks

Touch and be touched

At the kitchen sink I recut the stems floating in room temperature
    water and look just like my mother

Single moms do
Same-day delivery and smoke
Last cigarettes

These are for you

Cream colored with black buttons in the middle that are called
    anemones

II

PACIFIC POWER & LIGHT

One way to see is through
A Windowpane or
Disco Hama

Starlight hangs from a freshet in the front yard

Telephone lines or unagi race up Foster Road to an adductor in my
    childhood window

Bedroom hatcheries
Lit up at night by car lights and drop-offs
Awake in yellow sodium

Electric eels

The Coke in the fridge has a half-life

The grass is soaked and has never heard of us

The universe seems out of whack
If I can't call you
I can't call you

Huge green pages turn over beneath struggling carp and Jet Skis

I just stare at the pages

*

The rain is improvised
And makes everything smell better
Skinheads
And gooseberries

Tidal pressure and species pressure amount to big changes in the
    neighborhood over time and Johnson Creek

The TV on with the sound off

Plug-in footy pajamas are plugged in

A Wiffle ball
Swirls past fir trees
Food stamps and precut linoleum

A mignonette full of saline solution and local perspectives
Fender bender in the ground cover
Hoses instead of sprinklers

Everything else is something private not worth mentioning

Peed-in beds

Spaghetti out of cans

*

Free lunch programs
Float upstream through lichen and soft
Tap water
Battered and fried

Regrowth getting a late start in deep S.E.

The sound of ball bearings rubbed against other ball bearings

Bicycles stolen off the front porch
Skateboards stolen

Adults are like tide pools on the couch nodding off between shows
    they suck out the combos in the suppository

A crushed feeling of happiness and well-being

Late afternoon in the living room

Why not flush the toilet and write your name on water?

Lemon wedge wired to a lightbulb

String of pistils
Palmolive

With a salty or melon finish

*

High tide off 82nd & Foster
A quick upper for aromatic pathways
Without bus fare

Evergreens drip
Natural rewards onto crosswalks and curbs
An impressionistic intervention

Mom and Dad and the kids all drip

Sea palms wave to us in the water

Beta-blockers in the ocean spray

Neighborhood kids on bikes dart through spillage with no hands
    beneath streetlights and starbursts

Come home
New floods on the porch won't keep
The neighbors close by or away

It's impossible to tell where one good deed ends and another
    begins

Gentleness is all

Gentleness and candy

*

The trees aren't sick
They sip and process recreationals
Chlorophyll and spring again
In soft focus

For dinner broiled hamburgers and then *Cheers*

Wet blacktop receives us
Burnt yellow grass and the future
Will keep me company

Ants come inside when it rains and smell like peppermint

Something's not right

Oregon cherries slur their words and trail blossoms like damp
    cornflakes that slick up the sidewalks

A taste for granulated sugar
Bottles of domestic
And Theraflu

Milk teeth on the new fern did you see it?

I want to concentrate on you

III

RHODODENDRONS

A thought process
That remembers American robins
Microwaved nachos
And Coca-Cola

Boxing out the vinyl shake in a pastel wave of curdled cream with
   bubblegum highlights

Weevils pour out of pink trumpets

Named after people

They remember
Brown cans of Lemon Pledge and before the interstate
They remember age zero to twenty-one
Huffing glue in a Ziploc

A hybrid
Of cotton candy
And chemotherapy

Those shrubs were my friends but now they're hard to reach

Mid-March through mid-May

Each one has Saint Genet's face
Remembers sunlight
Shirts and skins

Teenage boys

In CinemaScope and Smell-O-Vision

MORRISON

Crushed Big Gulps
And drowned tall boys make up the new sedge
Alongside the newly improved
Crosswalks

Wet electronics
Pick out a signal-to-noise ratio that feels standard
Discounted produce in a bascule

Moss
Moss
Mosses

I don't live where I'm supposed to live

Salmon scale appliqué winks across the city's surface streets back
    and forth in horizontal shifts

Sequins
Overflow the passing lane
Where floating objects are big industry
And parade glitter

A bigleaf maple repairs its own DNA
Not changing color but staying
Green
As a caterpillar

Abandoned bicycles
Pedestrians and off-brand hypodermics

A second-line
Treatment for test roses
A comfort kit in stereo

The tape in the tape deck told me to describe what I see

The West Hills wave behind Big Pink

Nothing else does

TO A DEER IN THE WEST HILLS

A face that knows smaller faces
And can recognize group pressure
Around wet blinds
And babies

Each calling to each across a tennis court

Throwing up rose petals and weed killer

Black macadam
Is iridescent and looks like hooves
Liquid stanzas

You fan out in cohesive ripples of sunlight strung together by
    personal space and local secrets

Tongues disinfected with pink Quat

Rain settles
On your points and holes
Weather shuffled through a morning glory

Nose to nose
Siblings tucked inside
An envelope

Heartbeats melt
Back into parsley and horsetails
It's half you and half me

Singular and plural

Looking past private driveways and empty swimming pools

Little mouths spring up everywhere

BURNSIDE

Homeless pussy willows all bend
In the same direction like soft
Brown flame

En route to an egg roll
Or an edible bird's nest for a canvasback
Or butterball

Change doesn't arrive in any way that's recognizable that you can
know

Invasive rushes on one side and on the other tents in paradise

Waiting for a placebo in a hot lunch

The pussy willows have birdcalls
For drugs or danger
And an avant-garde
Family

These connections are unseen and lightly threaded through
grocery cart trash and alluvial fans

Swimming past wet cardboard
And nigiri

Downgraded to tenderness

Eyes staring into tinfoil
Eating and drinking
Dogshit

On one side is sleeping bags you can't climb out of and on the
    other side is 24-hour halogens

Local authors Charles Bukowski and Pablo Neruda wait for us

At either end

DANDELION

Grandpa Lion
In yellow sweater and buttons
Little butter lights
All aflame

Scattered across the puffed-out hay fever in the yard

A cup full of sunshine

A tight dissolve
Leaves lions swaying
Above a gold pin

Bees have a delivery system that translates hot summertime into
    dusted roe it looks like a soul

Redwood litter

An egg-shaped corolla

A fried egg
On the sidewalk gives
Birth to the Sahara

Old lions don't care about pain anymore because there isn't any

He just swallows and floats

DANDELION

Grandma Lion
Long fingers and long
Legs stretch out
For a drink in the goldenrod

Lights come back on one by one when you least expect it

They jump-start the grass

Glory
Opens the parachutes
Glory sends them out into the air

Lions look for thrips and stemware

A deal on earrings

Highlighter
Highlighter
Honeysuckle

She snaps a tablecloth above the yard
Her sharp little teeth collecting the corners
Into a star

Take my hand in your lion hand

Turn on a stem

CAMELLIAS

These side effects have soft edges
Strobe and visitation yellow
Sparklers stutter
Inside a speech impediment

Marshmallow gondolas

Time-traveling through a capsule or a contrasting petal color to
    end up right here where you are

Syntax
Burns a hole in the new
Four-square court

Across the street at the school
Kids eat Liquitex between cultivars
And OJ
From concentrate

Everything gets repeated over and over again is what tenderness is
    like

It genuflects inside your ear

At dusk
They are very chichi
In floral track lighting and
Dark green tulle

At dusk
They are very chichi
In floral track lighting and
Dark green tulle

RAINBOW SALMON

Hello string of pearls
Phosphorescent headlights
Bubble tea
Lite-Brites

Family structures worked up from dark matter and color samples
    are pure memory and crosscurrent

Survival through sequins

Ourselves in corners and fucking in corners
Weaving in and out of broken dishes
Clouds of Reddi-wip

Wet mouths open upstream

Sequins
Sequins
Vitamins

The grass hurts it's so green
The grass hurts
Behind our dark green
Ray-Bans

*

Finding a way
Inside is the hard part
We shimmy
Ourselves slipped inside a disinfected slipstream

Glowsticks broken in sloughs
Costume jewelry

Our brains increase through folds and microwaves past silt
    deposits and the recent past

Endless addition

Nothing ever happens how you want it to

Eating air
Breathing through disease and glucose
Ourselves a load of Pepto Bismol

We are tricked out in sunlight and sorry for everything

Scattered beneath black
Inner tubes and open arms
Open beneath

The native trees of Canada

*

Slick in leather jackets
The color of wet money
All candy-coated
All in a line
Ourselves nose to ass and hauling up escalators

Unraveling between a Billabong and mid-career Flavin

We translate Whirlpool into Maytag
Fingers laced in a church or wave
Eggs unbuttoned

Ourselves shoved through the eye of a needle

Scrambled inside a hole

The clouds in front of us and the clouds behind us are the same
    clouds

Fisting in a culvert
Nibbling the pulse off a bump
Spitting up newborns
In cursive loops

We ourselves are love

*

Dissolving
On our own tongues
Exploding in crystal and chrysanthemum
Off and on
Off and on in a hump

Reapply our lip glosses between takes and ripples

Ourselves the answer to every question

Poached in dry whites from Safeway
And pink peppercorns
From outer space

Everything else is still alive

The new streaming service is translucent and common running
    from early spring to late summer

We don't carry the souls of dead boys and girls

We shit milk and mop up the sky

Eyes
Made of jelly beans
Cheeks made of milk

*

Home
Licks us clean
Behind the ears and licks down our cowlicks
Tucks in loose shirttails
Mouths washed out with Dial

Open house for love poems
Open house for buttholes

Channels littered by centuries of lipsticked cigarettes and soft
    piles of descaled rainbow glitter

Ourselves muscled past jellied traffic then dumped at the
    Grab & Go

Genetic drift

Skittles tied off in cellophane

What we touch is ours
Fingered through a swimsuit
Told that we are pretty

Concentric circles pick up rose and slate
Laser green to lemon yellow
And coral and peony

BROADWAY

The last taxicab on earth glides past without any help
And breathes through crystal sac
Stoplights
Air in flukes

First dates performed in a panic
Telephone numbers
Connected by inhalants
And eyeliner

Sliding paper doors reveal a repeating mountain pattern coughing
    up western wear and pharmaceuticals

High heels and Diamond Brite

Dressed in black nail polish and a soft harness
Smoking cloves
Wrapped in whoever
Is close

Radios
Pick up passengers for free
And drop them downtown

We are beautiful and temporary

Mica in the coral

A replacement sluice parked along the curb in front of the club

MY BROTHER THE FLOWER

You put something on
For us to listen to that we have
Never heard before
Fritillaries graffiti
The upside of a honeydew

WOOF & WARP

A reflection off the surface of the public swimming pool
Sends out chlorine tracers

A blur on the plains

To-go bags in tree limbs motion to something you can't see

Substance in dreams
Substance in plastic wrap

There is a hole in my left eye through which everything dies and is
    born again

Blood in the center of the yolk curdles

Consonants
With new floaties swim
To the top of an antiseptic Slurpee

Squiggles
Tadpoles and circles

Lights disappear
Caribou disappear
What will I do when I can't read anymore?

I will sit in the living room and watch the neighbor's television

The neighbor's television is always on

*

If you knew how to relax
It might just go away all on its own
Messenger fluff
Blown off the head of
A dandelion

Sketchy in the afternoon
Sketchy in the way the afternoon zeros out

Cumulus
Cumulus
Contrails

Belief slides through it

Fields reiterate themselves like static cling before vanishing
    around a cul-de-sac

If I squint I can see the fiddleheads in the corner

Pincushions
Unfold to reveal a broken dash
Everything looks better flushed through a quick rinse of Visine

Certain words get farther away

Not lonely but more alone

WILLAMETTE

Home again
Home again
Lickity-
Split
A dreamed of

Piece of sea-green
Thread
With a door
On either end
It's like walking

Across a room
From here
To there
A brook trout
Inside a starry flounder

Inside a common
Minnow
Inside a goldfish
Rain in slo-mo
Disappears

Behind
Superman curtains
Hanging
In my first and only
Bedroom

A coho salmon
Inside a speckled dace
Inside a Pacific
Lamprey
Inside a pumpkinseed

Birds pick
Through shoal trickle
And liquid detergent
Interchangeable
And unknown

One thing
Doesn't always have
To be another
A northern flicker
On top of a western grebe

On top of a yellow
Warbler
On top of a kite
Methadone
And rosemary recycle

The swash
A rummage sale
A pancake supper
A turkey vulture
On top of a bufflehead

On top of a plover
On top of a clay-colored
Sparrow
My brother and I
Ollie over curbside

Runoff steelhead and plate
Tectonics
Above Washington Park
Hearts open
Alongside

The blissed-out
And local
Chum
Herons are
Depressed

Ampersand
And alluvial
A diminutive wave
Beneath a cabbage white
Beneath

A blue dasher
Beneath a little black stone fly
A schedule II
Damselfly
Should we just end

The call and try this
Again later
Eating crystal
Crystalline
Sedge

Styrofoam Styrofoam
Conscious
And verbal
Carpenter ant
Beneath a checkered white

Beneath a green darner
Beneath
A little yellow stone fly
Wild mint grows
Between

The Eastbank Esplanade
And the new
On-ramp
You can't cook
With it

It smells like cat piss
I wish I heard
Voices
Instead of
Whatever this is

I can't read
The messages
In the newly cut grass
Goo Balls
Stick

To macadam
Looping
Through Lovejoy Fountain
They don't
Spell anything

Cinder cone
Falling through mudstone
Falling through
Agates falling through
Fine fescue

A needle skips
Beneath
New traffic patterns
On the Banfield
Polyps

Scutch the weirs
The White Stag says *fuck you*
And was here
Before us
Alluvium

Falling through basalt
Falling through
Geodes falling
Through perennial
Ryegrass

Near Front and Salmon
And shocked bees
Fall onto
The sidewalk
Like applause

Or glazed fissions
And then
I was standing
In a backyard
In Princeton New Jersey

And couldn't recognize
Anything that was
An I
Or a part of me that I
Could know

Motion sensor
In the primrose I
Dropped in
Under the light that
Comes through

The
Trees
Everywhere
At
Dinnertime

All fucked up
Over Douglas firs
And Xanax
Nollies
And white matter

All fucked up
Over dogwoods
And Ketamine
No comply and the upper
Tributaries

All fucked up
Over Japanese maples
And Fentanyl
Fakies
And Chinook

All fucked up
Over Mount Hood
Floating
Above a varial
And a paper bag of paint thinner

All fucked up
Over Mount Hood
Floating
Above a shuvit
And a paper bag of lighter fluid

All fucked up
Over Mount Hood
Floating
Above a front foot impossible
And a fistful of brand-new silver Sharpies

Why not go home?

ACKNOWLEDGMENTS

The Guggenheim Foundation provided financial support during the writing of this book. The poem "Hawthorne" was first published in *Harper's Magazine*. "Broadway" was first published in *The New Republic*. The title "Blight of the Fumble Bee" is Gerry Mulligan's.

*

"Superior Florists" is for Hilton Als
"Broadway" is for Gus Van Sant
"To My Mother's Dogs" is for Nam Le

*

"Warp & Woof" and "Woof & Warp" are for Dr. Elizabeth Tegins

*

"Rainbow Salmon" is for Elizabeth Bishop

A NOTE ON THE TYPE

The text of this book was set in Freight
Text Pro Book, designed by Joshua Darden
(b. 1979) and published by GarageFonts in
2005. It was inspired by the "Dutch-taste"
school of typeface design and is considered
a transitional-style typeface. Legible,
stylish, and sturdy, Freight Text was
designed to be highly versatile, belonging
to a wide-ranging "superfamily" of fonts,
including many versions and weights.

Composed by North Market Street Graphics
Lancaster, Pennsylvania

Printed and bound by Friesens
Altona, Manitoba

Book design by Pei Loi Koay